His Death,
My Angel

Melissa Blue

AuthorHouse™
1663 Liberty Drive
Bloomington, IN 47403
www.authorhouse.com
Phone: 833-262-8899

This book is printed on acid-free paper.

ISBN: 978-1-4389-8871-9 (sc)

Print information available on the last page.

Published by AuthorHouse 01/05/2021

authorHOUSE®

DEDICATION

This book is dedicated to the loving memory of Willie Lee Blue (1925–1981) and of Lilla Lovett (1927–2009). I pray that a cure will be found for cancer so that the world does not have to continue to lose precious people to such a life-threatening disease. You both are deeply missed.

INTRODUCTION

I loved my grandfather. How could I not love him? He treated me like a little princess. I have a special place in my heart for my grandfather that is deep in nature and undeniable.

As I began to grow into a woman, I often thought about all the good times that we shared.

One day it just hit me like a ton of bricks that my grandfather was really and truly gone. While I was climbing the mountain of life, trying to get to the top and make the best out of my own life, I realized that I no longer had my grandfather by my side to climb with me.

I came to clearly see that I missed my hero and friend more than I ever knew. I made a decision to find a way to deal with the empty space in my heart by embracing the memories of the man that I loved the most, my granddaddy.

The world has produced many grandfathers over the centuries, but not just any man can be a granddad. One has to be caring, understanding, and protective to earn that title.

A granddad carries wisdom, and he thinks ahead to protect his own. When his family is hurting, he is there to comfort them and guard them from life's bullies. He has eyes as keen as an eagle's and instincts as sharp as a fox's.

Perhaps if my grandfather were still alive, he and I would have dinner together and watch a good movie on TV every now and then. I can think of many things that I would love to share with him.

Don't find it funny that big girls like me still daydream about the good old days with their granddads. Special events are very hard to come by. Life has many ups and downs, and when you can reflect on happy times, those thoughts can keep a smile on your face.

I have cried at times while wondering and asking God why he had to take my grandfather. He was my friend. I have needed him dearly over the years. Why did the horrible disease of cancer take over his lungs? "Why him?" I asked. If only he were alive, life would be so much easier.

As the years have gone by and as the hands of time tick away, I have learned that it is all right for me to miss Granddad. But it is not all right for me to dwell on the past or live in anger and heartbreak. I can't make Granddaddy come back, and I can't change what has happened to him. However, I can reflect upon the good times and use all of our joyous moments as fuel for the future.

I know that God allowed me to have precious memories to remind me of the love that Granddad and I shared. We had some great times.

There are so many memories of my grandfather that absolutely put a smile on my face. I try to think of the good times instead of the sad ones.

I can still remember being a little girl sitting on my granddaddy's lap while watching our favorite television shows. His favorite chair was the recliner. Believe me when I say that my granddaddy got his money's worth from his recliner. I don't recall Granddad sitting in any chair other than that recliner except for the dining room chairs, and even then he had a favorite chair at the table.

My grandfather would sit in the recliner with his legs extended, and he always had a toothpick in his mouth. The toothpick was the grand finale for every meal.

He and I would sit in that chair and laugh so hard at the *Little Rascals*. We loved to watch Alfalfa, Buckwheat, and Spanky. Granddaddy and I hardly ever missed an episode of *Shirley Temple Theater*, the western *Gunsmoke*, or wrestling.

When Granddad's sleepiness began to really get to him, his head would hang down low so that his chin would nearly touch his chest.

Slobber would hang and drop from his bottom lip. "Yuck," I would say, and then it would be time for me to get off of his lap. I didn't want any slobber on me! Sometimes I would nudge him and tell him to wake up before the slobber reached the dripping point. He would immediately sip it up and act as if he hadn't been asleep. I know that it is a little gross, the slobbering and all, but at the same time it made for some very memorable moments.

My grandfather always had a cap on his head, and as he fell asleep, the cap would fall off and land on the floor. I would pick up the cap and gently put it on his head, trying not to wake him, but eventually it would fall on the floor again.

I found myself watching him while he slept. He was entertaining to watch because his head bobbed up and down when he fell asleep. Funny stuff!

I suppose you can say that I was kind of spoiled by both my grandmother and my grandfather, but Granddad is the one who loved to show me off. He would call me his "munk munk." Who knows what that meant, but that was his nickname for me.

I could not wait for the walk up the hill to Mr. Willie Edward's candy store. The store was a wooden house-like structure that was supported by bricks at the foundation. There were all kinds of candy. Granddaddy would say to me, "Get whatever you want." I would say, "OK!" with a huge smile on my face. I would then reach into one of the jars and pull out a handful of candy. I liked the saltwater taffy the most. After getting my goodies, which usually included candy, chips, and a soda, Granddaddy and I would walk back home.

Granddaddy used to work at a lumberyard that was right next door to our Main Street home. On the days that I had no school, I would walk next door to visit my granddad at work if he had not came home for lunch first.

Everyone knew me at the lumberyard because I was Willie's granddaughter.

I would get a soda and chips from the storefront of the lumberyard, and then I would sit in the area where the wood was sawed and watch my grandfather work. While sitting on a hard wooden bench, I would observe customers coming in and going out of the facility and watch the forklifts maneuver. Eventually my grandfather or one of his friends would ask me if I wanted a ride on the forklift, and of course I would say yes. I felt as if I were working too. Those were the good old days.

A Healing Moment

Once, my grandfather was having pain in one of his legs, and he could hardly move it without aching. My grandmother tried all that she could to comfort him. I believe that my grandmother noticed my concern for my grandfather because she asked me to pray for his leg. I have no idea how old I was at that time, but if I were to guess, I would say about six or seven years old. I recall putting one of my hands on Granddaddy's leg and closing my eyes tightly. I opened my mouth, and the words of faith began to flow from my lips as I asked God to heal my grandfather's leg. I was sincere with my prayer request because I really wanted Granddaddy to feel better.

After praying, I opened my eyes and removed my hand from the top of his leg. My hand was very warm, and a tingling sensation ran through my fingers.

A short time afterward, I looked at my grandfather and saw that his face was lit up with a look of amazement. My grandmother asked him, "How does your leg feel?" He moved his leg up and down with a little bit more ease and said to her, "It feels better." We all thanked God in our own little way for that healing moment.

It made my heart proud to know that I was used by God to help my grandfather. To me, it was a miracle. My grandmother will never forget that; she still speaks of it once in a blue moon.

Granddaddy really looked out for me. I don't think that he could stand to see me cry. On occasion, I would spend the day or weekend with my father and his family, so there were times when I would sit and wait for my father to come by the house to pick me up. I recall standing at the window with my bags packed, waiting and waiting. I went to the door every time I thought I saw a car that resembled my father's, but most of the time it was only my imagination.

I sat for hours, it seemed, and no one would come to pick me up all day long. I could not help but cry from heartache. I was heartbroken. Granddad would get so angry when my dad did that to me, and he had no problem telling people about themselves on my behalf. Granddad and my grandmother would comfort me to try and rid me of my broken heart.

The stories of my grandfather could go on and on, but there is one more memory in particular that I think of often. I remember feeling so grown up in this story.

In the mornings, Granddad had to have a nice-sized breakfast. His breakfast would usually consist of toast, eggs, grits, bacon, and a cup of coffee. I would sit at the table, waiting for my own plate of food. I was barely big enough to put my elbows on the table. The highlight of my breakfast was coffee. I was pretty young to be drinking coffee, but I loved it. Granddaddy put tons of sugar in his coffee, and then he would pour a little bit of coffee on a saucer for me. I blew on it, turned the saucer up to my mouth, and sipped away. I thought I was a little lady, sipping coffee with my breakfast.

Granddaddy started to get ill when I was about eight years old. He didn't want me to know what was going on with him. He really tried to keep his illness a secret when it came to me. Granddad was not impressed with the thought of my seeing him dying.

Cancer was eating away at him slowly. All of those years of inhaling cigar tobacco had finally caught up with him. His lungs could no longer fight against the invasion of the deadly disease.

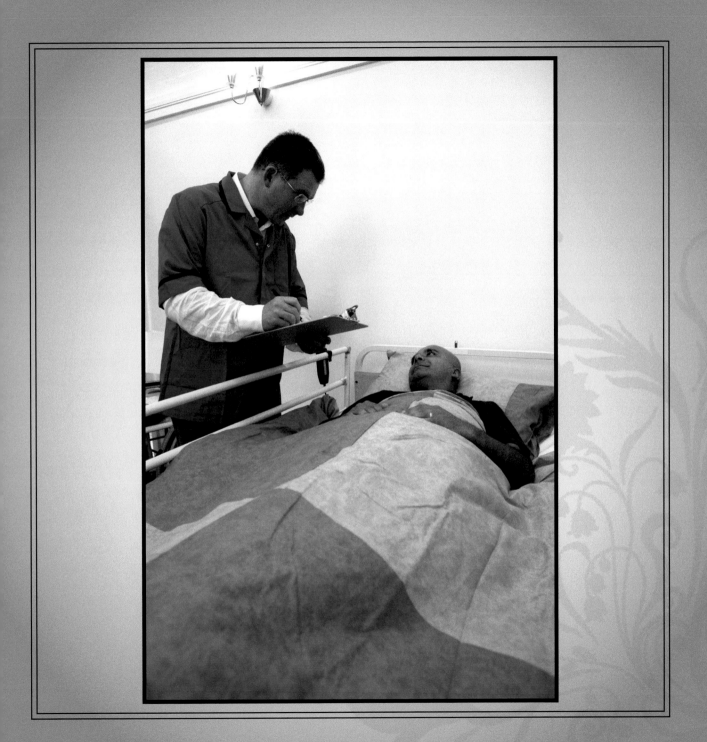

During his last days, I hardly saw him. He wanted to keep my memories of him joyous. My mother, grandmother, and I would go to the Veterans Hospital to visit him. The more ill he became, the shorter my bedside visits were. Soon it got to the point that I was not allowed in his hospital room. A short time after that, he passed.

I didn't really react to the news. I don't remember crying. Perhaps I was already prepared in my heart. I'm not sure why I hardly reacted. I had the choice of whether to go to Granddad's funeral, but I chose not to attend. I knew that if I went to the funeral, it would be hard for me, so I stayed with one of my adult cousins instead.

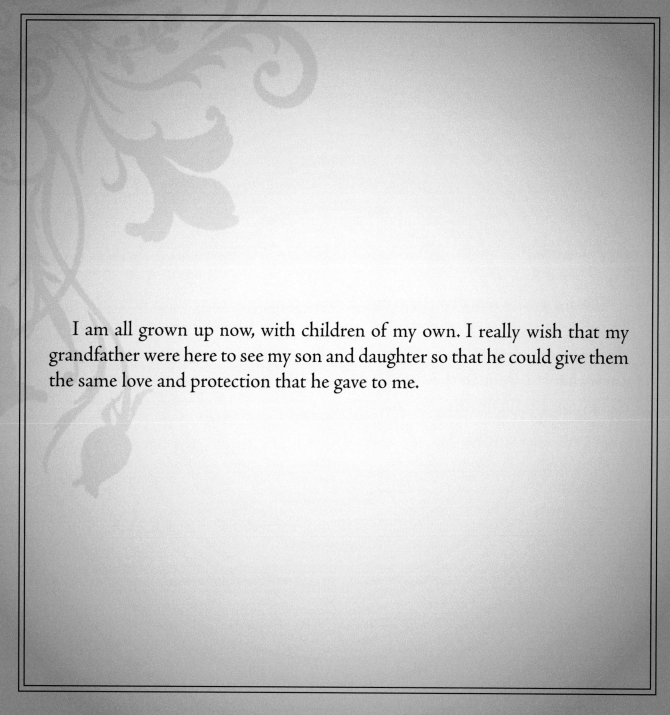

I am all grown up now, with children of my own. I really wish that my grandfather were here to see my son and daughter so that he could give them the same love and protection that he gave to me.

I've gone through a lot in my days. When I feel sad or lonely, I know that it's Granddaddy who helps comfort me; he's my angel. I may not be able to see him physically, but somehow I can feel his love when it matters the most.

One day, there will be a love that reminds me of the love Granddaddy provided. I do long for that kind of love again. Not very often do you find a person who allows you to feel safe and secure. I believe that my grandfather and God have already made arrangements for me to be as happy as I was when he was alive. That happiness is on its way—I just know it. For now I'll rest in the arms of God and allow him to heal my every wound and wipe away all of my tears.

CONCLUSION

To all of you who have lost a loved one to the horrible disease of cancer or for any other reason, I encourage you to share the stories of your deceased loved ones as a form of healing. Your story could help someone else through his or her personal trials.

Cherish the ones you love and those who love you. Real love and friendship are hard to find, so embrace love and friendship while you are yet living. Value your grandparents, for they possess a wisdom that can be worth more than a pot of gold.

The story that you just read is a true story. I am "Lisa," the little girl in this story; "Lisa" is a nickname. I thank you for reading about my experience. Since the creation of this manuscript, my dear and precious grandmother passed away due to cancer. This book is also dedicated to her. Now I have two angels watching over me.

Please share this book with a friend, a family member, or someone else in need of healing.

—Melissa Blue

Printed in the United States
By Bookmasters